How to Draw More
MANGA

How to Draw More
MANGA

Katy Coope

an imprint of
■SCHOLASTIC
www.scholastic.com

Author: Katy Coope

Designed and produced by
D&S Books Ltd.,
Kerswell, Parkham Ash,
Bideford, Devon, EX39 5PR, U.K.

© 2003 D&S Books Ltd.

an imprint of
■SCHOLASTIC
www.scholastic.com

Scholastic and Tangerine Press and associated logos are trademarks of Scholastic Inc.

Published by Tangerine Press, an imprint of Scholastic Inc., 557 Broadway, New York, NY 10012

10 9 8 7 6 5 4 3 2 1

ISBN: 0-439-58560-0

Printed and bound in China

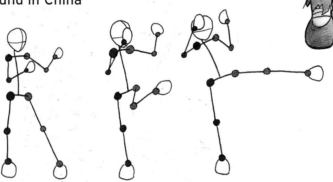

Creative director: Sarah King
Project editor: Clare Haworth-Maden
Designer: Axis Design Editions

Contents

Introduction

One of the things that people love about Manga and Anime are the variety of wild character designs. But how do you create them?

In this book, you're going to design your own characters. You're going to draw characters with different kinds of faces, clothes, accessories, and cool animal friends. And you'll learn to put them in cool poses and scenes.

Everyone has his or her own way of designing characters. The most important thing is to be creative! One of the best places to start is with something called a "character concept."

Although it sounds complicated, it's nothing to be afraid of. A character concept is a basic idea of who your character is, and what he or she looks like. The way someone looks often gives you a clue about his or her personality.

Inspiration can come from anywhere, and with a little bit of practice you can make your very own characters! Try thinking about your favorite Anime or Manga movie, book, comic, show, or video game. Do you have a favorite character? If so, what is it about that character that you really like?

For instance, create a pair of characters, a boy and a girl with these character concepts:
• a quiet, mysterious boy with martial-arts skills and a secret past
• a bubbly, smart schoolgirl who is granted special powers

Your concepts can be as simple as this or as complicated as you want. As you think about your concepts, you'll probably start getting ideas about what your characters look like . So start thinking about your character concept, grab your pencil, and let's go!

Faces & Bodies

1

When you're creating a character, there are two things to keep in mind: the way they look and the way they dress. Unless they have a special costume, most people don't dress the same way all of the time. So start with how a character looks. There are a lot of things you can vary to show different types and styles of characters, whether they're young or old, tall or short, cute or dangerous-looking. Let's start with the basic face.

Face Shapes

Although most character's faces are similar in shape, they vary slightly. When you're drawing a face, start with a basic shape.

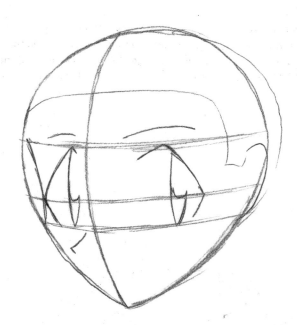

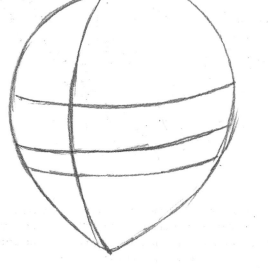

1 Start off with a pointed egg shape, the point being the chin. Work very lightly as you're going to be erasing a lot of the lines. Draw a line up the center to cut it in half, as if it has been drawn curved around the egg. Draw eye lines, one that cuts the halves into quarters, one a little below that, and one a bit farther above the center line. The top and bottom lines show you the size of the eyes.

2 Start drawing in the basic features. Draw the top of the eye first, going up to the top eye line, down to the middle, and curving back in toward the bottom eye line. The light is coming from the top right in this drawing, so draw a backward "J" shape for the iris and pupil, and another one inside that to make the shine. Add eyebrows, and a nose like a checkmark turned on its end. Draw in a hint of the ear and the hair line. (Add another line for the back of the head as well.) Start defining the shape of the actual face with an inward curve on the side of the face farthest away from the light (top right), going from the top eye line to the bottom.

3 Add more details and thicken the outside lines of the eyes. Then draw in the pupils and a little shadow in the irises. Give your character a mouth and some hair. (Large bangs and spiky hair is very stylish.) Define the shape of the face, following the lines of the egg to show the shape of the chin. When you have done that, add the neck.

4 Draw in the rest of the details, and go over the most important lines again with your pencil so you can see them better. Draw in the blush lines, some more lines for the hair, a jagged hairline, the shape of the eyebrows, the hair at the back of the head, and the details of the ear.

5 The next step is to ink it all in. Use a thin pen for the delicate details on the eyes, blush lines, eyebrows, and mouth. Use a medium-sized pen for other details. Then erase all of the pencil lines and go around the outside of the drawing again with a thick pen.

6 Once you've drawn the face, you can color it in. You can use any skin color for this, but you can add interest with a much darker shade on one of the bangs. There's more information about coloring your characters on Page 54.

Now you've drawn a basic face!
Begin thinking about your character's personality as you make changes to the basic face shape.

One of the first things you can change is the shape of the chin. Do you want it pointed or not?

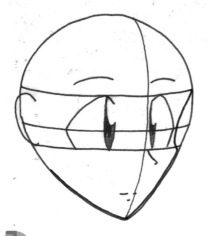 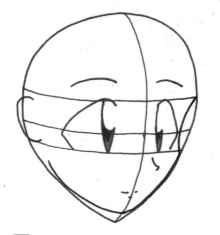 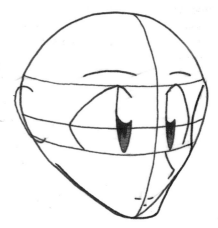

1 Here the chin follows the shape of the egg very close. But what if you don't want a pointed chin?

2 You can round off the chin to make a soft curve. (This makes the character look younger.) Or maybe you want a more defined chin?

3 Make the chin line come out level with the point of the egg, and then curve it back into the jaw line. This variation makes the character look more adult.

Here are some other possible variations.

The first thing to do is stretch the egg shape. You can draw it taller and thinner.

Or you can make it shorter and fatter. Stretch the shape of the egg shown in Step 1 on Page 8.

If you want your character to have a more defined chin, all you have to do is change the basic face shape on the top or bottom of the egg shape, like these two faces.

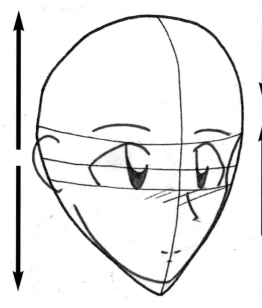 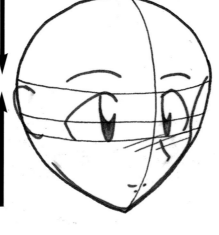

The bottom of the egg shape is cut off to make it flat. Drawing a square chin makes a character look older and more masculine.

You can give male characters beards or moustaches, and if you want to make characters look older, give them a few wrinkles. Add makeup to make female characters look more grown-up.

Here are a few more examples of different faces. What sort of characters do you think they are? See if you can copy them. Then draw some different faces of your own!

Bodies

We've seen how faces affect a character's personality, but how about bodies? Is a character tall or short? Young or old? Thin or heavy? It's completely up to you!

When you're drawing bodies, remember they're built from very basic shapes. To change someone's build, alter some of these shapes.

Let's start with a basic, simple figure.

1. Start with a stick figure, with the face shape drawn in and circles to show where the joints will be. You can skip this stage when you become more confident, but it's helpful for planning poses.

2. Now draw the basic shapes. Draw in the face and chin to make sure that the neck is in the right place. Put in some bigger circles for the joints. Draw the arms and legs so they look like cylinders, making them a little fatter in the middle. Try to draw this step as accurate as you can because everything else will be based on it.

3. Add more details to the face and draw in the clothes, making them hang off the body. Draw in the body, based on the shapes you drew in Step 2 and smoothing them out. Don't worry if something doesn't look quite right. You can always erase it or draw more lines over the top until you get it right.

4. Add more details. If there are lines you don't want, go over the lines you want to keep, pressing down with your pencil a little harder to make them clearer.

5. Ink the character.

6. Then color it in.

Now change the basic figure.

To change the way a character is built, alter the first couple of steps in the original figure. Whenever you're drawing figures with their arms hanging down by their sides, try to make the elbows roughly level with the waist and the hands fall about halfway down the upper legs. Try to remember this because it'll help make the proportions look right.

This is the basic figure.

If you want a big, bulky character, draw bigger shapes that are further apart.

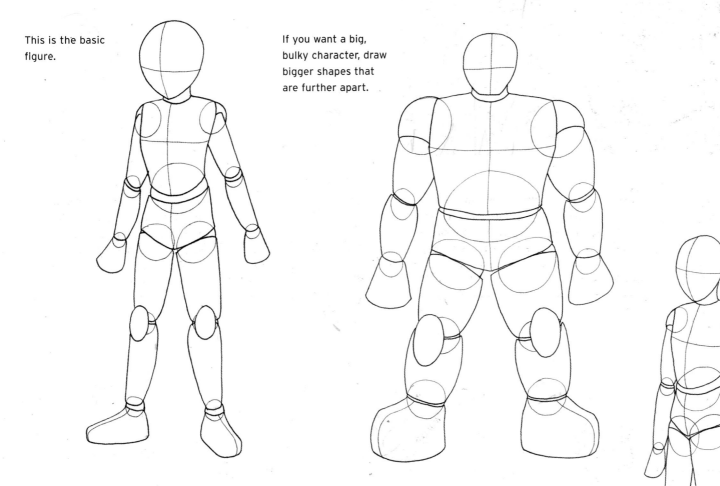

See the difference? The bulky character has much wider shoulders and hips, as well as a smaller head in relation to his body. The shapes used for his arms and legs are thicker and more curved. The joint circles are a lot bigger, too, especially the ones at the shoulders that show muscle definition. (Use one of the square-jawed face shapes for this figure because it tends to suit big, heavy characters.)

Or draw a tall, thin character.

Even though the shapes of the arms and legs aren't much thinner than in the basic figure, they're a lot longer. The shoulders are about the same size, but the torso is elongated. Most of the difference in height is due to the length of the legs. (Draw a taller, thinner head shape for this figure.)

People usually grow taller as they get older, but a character with broad shoulders will look more grown-up, too.

Here are some female body shapes.

There are a few differences between the male figure and the female figure, mainly in the torso and lower body. Female characters have narrower shoulders, wider hips, and smaller waists. If the character is a young female, the differences between male and female will be less obvious.

Change a female character's build by drawing more curves.

Or drawing them tall and willowy.

Here are some characters with different faces and body types. See how the changes in the basic body enhance the character's personality.

Details

Now that you have drawn basic face and body shapes, try drawing more details like the eyes.

Eyes

There are a lot of ways to draw eyes. The style of the eyes is a great way to identify the illustrator. If you look at your favorite Anime and Manga characters, you'll see the different artistic styles.

A basic eye is very simple to draw.

1 Draw in the face guidelines as you did on Page 8.

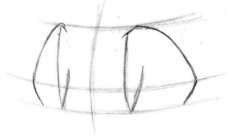 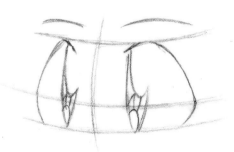 

2 Draw curves from the top eye line to the middle one. Then curve in to the bottom eye line. Draw backward "J"s for the irises. The gaps are drawn on the side where the light is coming from. In this case the light is coming from the top right.

3 Draw in the shines and add the pupils and shadows. (Add more shine if you want.) Draw in the eyebrows (simple slightly curved lines over the eyes).

4 Thicken the outside line of the eyes to shade the pupils and eye socket. You can also draw eyelashes. Draw eyelashes where the eye curves toward the bottom lines. This will make your character look feminine.

There are also a lot of ways to change eyes. You can apply these variations to any style. Try some ideas with the style that we just drew.

The first big thing to consider is how large the eyes should be. Eye size reveals lots about personality, with bigger eyes often making people look younger, cuter, or more innocent. The size of the eyes will also change the face shape a little.

Makes quite a difference, doesn't it? As you can see, very big eyes make the face look even more cartoonlike and work best for characters who are meant to be really cute.

Now, think about is the basic shape of the eyes. Are they taller than they are wide or the other way around?

Taller eyes make a character look cuter.

Change the corner position of the eyes to make them look slanted.

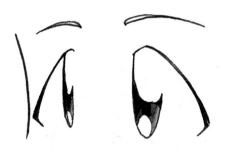

Upward-slanting eyes make a character look mysterious, and a lot of bad guys are given narrow, slanted eyes. Upward-slanting eyes make a character look very awake. If the eyes slant down, a character looks sad.

The line around the outside of the eyes can be changed, too. It can be curved or pointed . . .

. . . thick or thin.

Here are some different ways to draw eyelashes.

In general, the more eyelashes, and the more curved the eyelashes are, the more feminine a character will look.

Here are some more eye variations to try . . .

Making changes to the iris or pupil area will affect the mood and personality of a character. If the iris is larger, a character looks very cute, especially if you draw a lot of shine.

There are hundreds of styles to draw for eyes (just take a look at some of your favorite Anime and Manga characters for ideas).

Noses

The nose is an easy detail to change. You'll need to decide how big it is. Is it straight or turned up? Big or little?

Very small and turned-up noses tend to look cute and feminine.

Hair

Hair is important, too. Change the hair style according to a character's fashion and personal style. Here are some hair styles to think about: Does your character have natural-colored hair (like blond, brown, or black), or a wild color (like blue, green, purple, or pink)? Do bangs hang in your character's eyes? Is your character's hair long or short, straight, or curly; hanging free or tied back; neat or scruffy? Try to draw these hair styles. Think about what kind of personality they go with. The character's eyes are drawn closed so you can concentrate on the hair.

Final Details

Final details will make your character stand out. Distinctive features like unusual eye colors and special markings will add style. If your character is not human, draw pointed ears on her. Details like these will change your character from everyday to fantasy. Try drawing a fantasy character, but add details like a tail or even wings. (For more ideas, see the "Animals" chapter, on Page 48.)

You've learned a lot of things about drawing a character. If you haven't started drawing yet, try drawing a character based on your character concept. Try drawing a lot of versions of your character until you find one that works for you. And don't forget to add a lot of imagination.

Introducing Drei and Kara

Now, let's put it all together. Here are two completed characters based on character concepts.

The first thing you'll want to do is give your characters names. The names of these characters are Drei and Kara.

Drei, the boy, is a little tall and thin. He seems to be a little mysterious since his eyes are slightly smaller and more slanted. Since he is male, he needs a more defined chin. He has a different style so the wild, blue hair and violet eyes add to his sense of style. To add further to the mysterious look a few markings were added.

On the other hand, Kara, the girl, is a little shorter with large eyes and a small nose, making her look cute and bubbly. Her hair style with the ponytails adds to her bubbly personality. She has natural colored hair and eyes to show the difference between the two character's personalities.

So that's how you design a basic character. First start with your character concept. Then draw your basic face and body shapes, and then add the final details.

Clothes & Accessories

2

Fabric

How you draw fabric will make clothing look realistic. Make sure to add fabric folds, stretches, creases, and hangs. If you put folds in clothes in the right places, it will look a lot better. Look at photographs and your own clothes to see how fabric behaves. Shading and highlighting fabric will make it look even more realistic.

Drawing fabric from real life is a good way to practice. Even though you're drawing Manga characters, drawing from real life is a great way to make your characters look more realistic.

Practice drawing fabric that is bunched up, folded, or stretched. Remember practice is what will make you good at drawing characters.

More details like seams, fastenings, and pockets will make clothes look realistic. For example, these jeans look okay.

But, these look more like jeans because of the details that were added.

To give style to your character's clothes and add interest, draw colored trim, patterns, logos, and different textured fabric.

Shading Different Textures

Creating a textured fabric can be very time-consuming if you try to show every detail. To create ribbed fabric, like corduroy, start with a medium color. Then, draw shadow lines a little darker than the main color. Finally, use a lighter color to create the highlights (where the light hits first).

Rough fabric, like denim is created using a very sharp pencil to pick up the "grain" of the paper. If you're using good-quality paper, a blunt pencil works, too.

Now decide how your character is going to dress.

Here are some great ideas for different types of clothing.

To draw a hooded top, add folded fabric to the shoulders and a couple of draw strings.

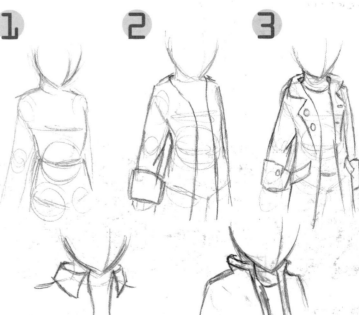

Draw a coat hanging off the body. Add details like cuffs, a collar, and buttons. Change the shape of the collar or take away the cuffs to create a different style of coat.

Jewelry and watches are a fast and easy way to add style and accessories for your characters. Use basic shapes plus a few details for different styles.

23

To make a button, draw a circle. Add a smaller circle inside to show the rim. Then add buttonholes and small lines to indicate thread.

Create a chain by drawing a row of connected circles. If you want to make the chain look more realistic, draw the links.

For a zipper, draw two parallel lines. Then divide it into little boxes for the teeth and add a zipper pull.

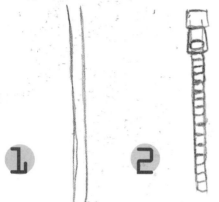

Shoes can be drawn simple or more complicated. For simple shoes and sneakers, draw a basic foot shape. Smooth it out and draw the shoe shape. Then add the details of laces and designs.

   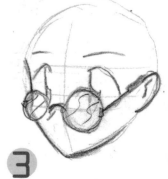

Bags and glasses are easy accessories to draw.

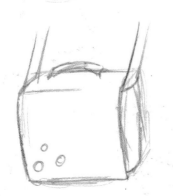   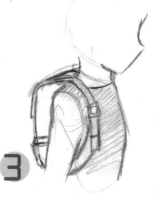

Costume ideas come from movies, plays, books, comics, and magazines, as well as from your favorite Anime or Manga.

Samurai

One of the most popular settings for Anime and Manga is the time of the samurai, in feudal Japan. Kimonos, swords, and martial arts are great costumes for a historical atmosphere. Here are the characters, Drei and Kara in samurai-style costumes.

Look at some books about the time period of the samurai for accurate details. The clothing should be loose, so the characters can move easily. Zippers were not a part of this time period. The fastenings should be simple. A lot of warriors wore their own designs on their kimonos, so have fun thinking up symbols and designs for your characters.

Kimono tops and sandals are drawn like this.

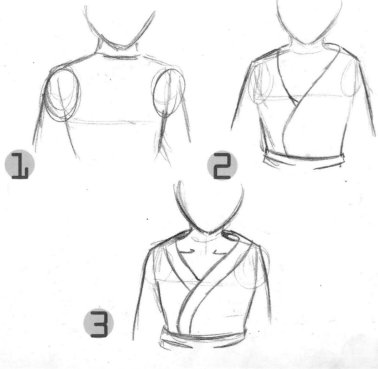

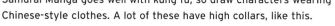

A lot of characters in this kind of setting carry weapons, which are really easy to draw. A basic Japanese-style sword is drawn like this.

1 Draw a thin cylinder for the hilt (handle), making sure it's long enough to fit both hands. Draw the shape of the blade, so it curves slightly. The point of the blade is on one edge instead of between two, like a knight's sword. The blade will be on the edge that curves up to the point.

2 Draw a circular handguard. (Because we're drawing the sword at an angle, this should be oval.) Add some details to the blade and hilt.

Drawing spears and other weapons is just as easy as drawing the rest of the character. Keep using the basic shapes.

3 Add more details, such as engraving on the handguard and blade. Then ink it in and shade it so the sword's metal looks shiny.

Samurai Manga goes well with kung fu, so draw characters wearing Chinese-style clothes. A lot of these have high collars, like this.

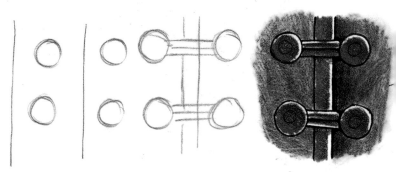

Add embroidery and different types of details to this kind of clothing. Details are created with circles, lines, and groups of teardrop shapes. Customize swords with tassels and different-shaped handguards.

The characters in historical settings often have the same sort of romantic, fantasy feel as characters from stories of the knights of the round table and Robin Hood.

Fantasy

Drei and Kara look great in sword-and-sorcery costumes.

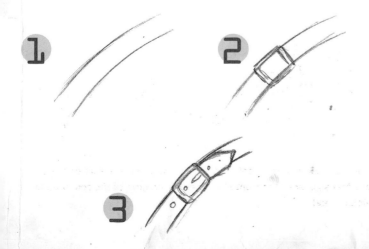

Fantasy settings are a lot of fun to draw. Look at the fantasy characters shown on Page 15 for more ideas.

Draw clothes for a fantasy by adding folds of fabric, like those on Kara's cloak or these boots.

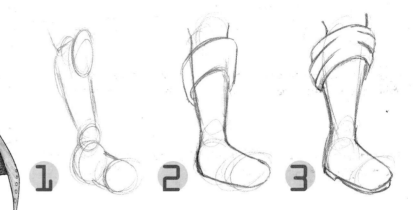

Or draw stiff gloves.

Draw belts and wraps with simple parallel lines.

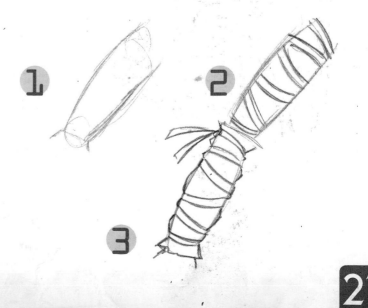

Bows and arrows make great accessories in this time period.

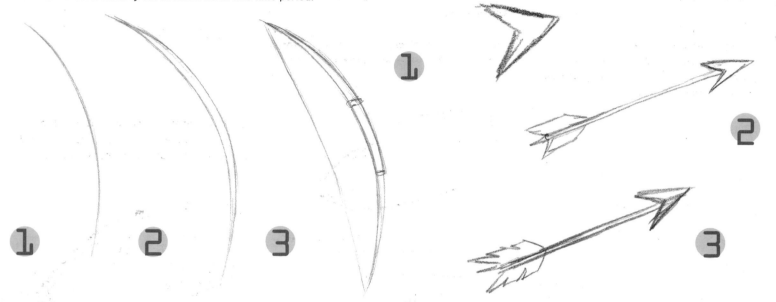

Armor is a little more complicated to draw, but keep basic shapes in mind when drawing. Create the armor shapes with smooth curves and straight lines over the shapes of the face and body, as shown below.

For a helmet, use smooth curves and straight lines. If you want it to be more ornate, add trim and decoration for a personal touch.

Chain mail is a cool detail and pretty easy to draw.

Start by drawing a set of lines around the body part that has chain mail. Then draw in "scales" by drawing a lot of little "U" shapes. Now ink and color in the chain mail.

1

2

3

4

There are lots of different ways to draw shiny metal. Indicate shiny metal either by inking or coloring it in.

This is the simplest way. Draw very thin, broken lines around the edge, where the light hits it.

Add some round shine lines, as you would for eyes. This kind of shine works best on rounded metal objects.

For a flat metal object, draw the shine running in a curve across the surface, but make it straight if you like.

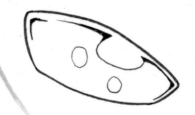

Use color to show these effects. The only difference is you color everything except the shiny area (highlight). The shading should be darker near the lines and lighter in the middle.

Draw small lines from the edge toward the middle with varying pressure. Press down hard at the beginning of the line, but very light at the end.

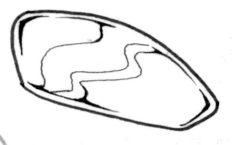

Some artists leave gaps in the outline of the metal to show the light hitting it.

Use metal for fantasy settings, but it's good for futuristic scenes, too.

Science Fiction

1

2

3

Here are Kara and Drei drawn in sci-fi-style costumes. Kara is wearing a futuristic armor and shiny clothes. Drei's costume looks like a modern day outfit, and his headband is exchanged for a pair of goggles.

Creating futuristic gadgets is easy and a lot of fun. Draw basic shapes and keep adding details, like wires and buttons.

4

Wires are really easy. Draw curved cylinders and add lots of curved lines to show covered wire.

Alien lettering adds a very futuristic detail to these types of gadgets.

Leave a rectangle where you want the letters to go. Then divide that into smaller blocks for each letter. To create the actual letters, shade in corners, squares, or round areas with the background color. Then color them in with a bright color.

1

2

3

Draw a bundle of wire like this.

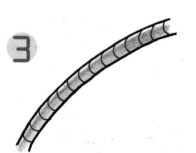

Sci-fi armor is often made of different-shaped plates with small gaps between them, and is not quite as shiny as other armor.

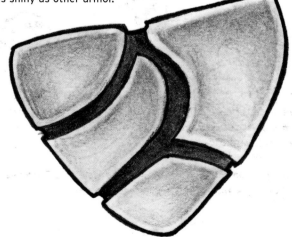

Plugs can be drawn using simple shapes.

Hands

Drawing hands looks difficult, but just keep the simple shapes in mind.

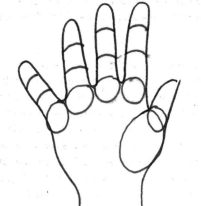

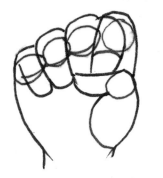

Remember draw hands with the fingers pointing away from each other when your hand is naturally open, and toward each other when closed. Open and close your hand to see the different positions.

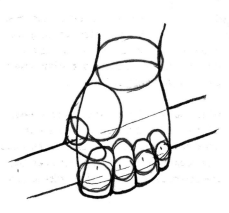

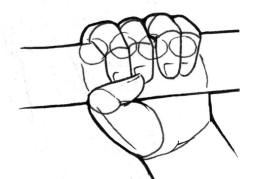

Draw a hand with a lot of basic shapes. Arrange the shapes around the object your character is holding. Remember most people's palms aren't square. The edge where the fingers start is sloped. The longest side is by the thumb. Understanding this will make the hands look more realistic and the wrists more natural.

Your characters can hold small items like cards between their fingers, as well as, gripping large things with their whole hand.

If you have trouble drawing a hand doing what you want, look at your own. Spend time drawing your hands, making your drawing as detailed and accurate as possible. Practice will help improve your drawing a lot.

Choosing Your Design

Think about your character concept. It's time to decide what style of clothes you want on your characters.

Drei and Kara are in the same story, and the story is set in modern times. Therefore, their clothes are not costumes. They are both wearing modern clothes, but Drei is wearing a Chinese-style shirt. The blue markings on his face and arms give him a very different style from Kara.

Notice how the color of these character's clothes add to their personalities. Drei's colors are a little darker and less bright than Kara's, who is a bubbly, happy person. Kara's outfit is mainly blue and purple which are calm colors. This shows she is relaxed and laid-back. Red is better for active characters. The gold trim on Drei's top gives him a noble style, but his jeans and white headband balance the noble impression.

Drei has simple accessories, but the details on his gloves give him a cool style. Kara is wearing cute jewelry. The feather shows she might have a pet or might have just found a bird.

When you pick clothes for your characters, think about his or her personality and the world in which he or she lives. Also think about what looks cool to you. And remember, your characters can have as many outfits as you want.

Poses & Action

Poses and actions are how you animate your characters. When you're drawing your characters, you could show them standing, walking, or just moving their arms. Your characters can be doing whatever you like. Take a closer look at some of the things characters usually do.

Standing

How a character stands says a lot about his or her personality.

This character looks happy and laid-back. His shoulders are relaxed, and curved down. HIs legs are apart, but straight, and his arms are slightly bent. His head is up, which usually shows confidence.

In this posture the same character looks less happy. His shoulders are hunched, and he is bent over. His hands are in his pockets, which suggests that he's hiding something. His head is tilted down, which implies shame or guilt, as does looking down. His feet are closer together and his legs are a little bent, which makes him look uneasy or sad.

Here are more stick figures in different standing positions. Try drawing your characters in these positions. Think about the emotion or personality these positions suggest as you draw.

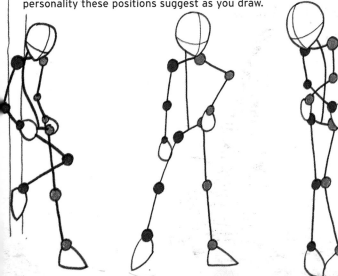

When you have practiced drawing your character standing, draw him or her standing on a surface. To make characters look like they are standing on a surface, rather than floating in space, the character's feet need to look as if they are on the surface.

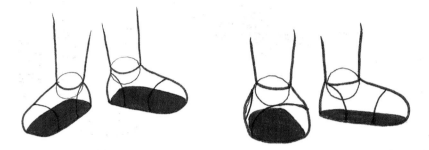

Normally, you wouldn't draw the soles of the feet, but if it helps you position the feet correctly, draw the soles in the same position as the surface the character is standing on.

Create a sidewalk by drawing a row of slanted squares with rectangles along the edge, as shown below.

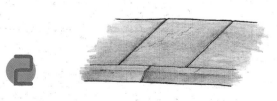

For the corners, draw the rectangles getting narrower as they round the corner and disappear into the sidewalk. Use broken lines and chipped areas to show cracks for a more realistic.

To create bricks, draw a horizontal grid. Above each line of the grid draw wobbly lines to indicate the bricks and mortar. Note that the bricks are not in line with the row below or above. Then ink it. Color in the bricks using an orange-red color. Add texture with a dark red or brown, using the side of the lead.

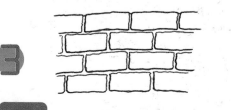

Draw a wooden surface by dividing the background into stripes. Then fill the stripes with thin, wavy lines. Add a few spirals to show the knots in the wood.

Color in the wooden surface with ink following the wavy lines. Apply a brown color. Color a base of brown and draw in the texture with a dark brown.

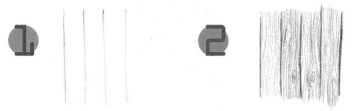

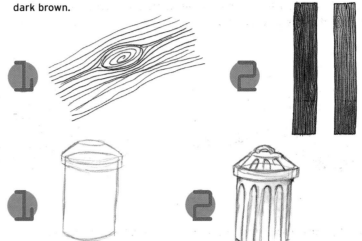

Draw basic objects by breaking them into basic shapes. Draw the garbage can from a cylinder and part of a cone. The sign is created from rectangles. Look at all the things in your environment. See if you can break them down into basic shapes and draw them.

Now that you have mastered some basic backgrounds, add your characters. Try drawing a group of characters with different personalities. Show the difference between them in the way they are standing.

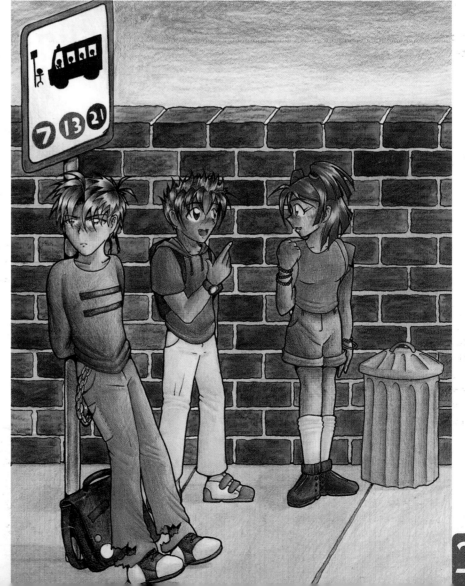

37

Walking

Let's get things moving by drawing people walking. Just like how you stand shows your attitude, so does how you walk. Let's start with the basics.

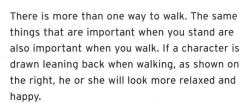

There is more than one way to walk. The same things that are important when you stand are also important when you walk. If a character is drawn leaning back when walking, as shown on the right, he or she will look more relaxed and happy.

If characters are bending forward, they look in a hurry or depressed, depending on where they're looking and what they're doing with their arms.

Kara and Drei are walking down a path and talking. Kara looks relaxed, and is looking around her as she walks. Drei is more focused, and is looking at Kara while they talk. A simple background of grass and trees is a great scene for this type of action. Add some shadows, which should be shown moving away from the light wherever anything solid touches the ground.

Trees

1 Draw a tree starting with a distorted cylinder for the trunk.

2 Then add some thinner cylinders at the top for branches. Draw some bumps on the trunk and a jagged line for the grass.

3 Draw a bunch of wobbly balls over the ends of the branches. Then add more behind them until you think you have enough.

4 Draw a jagged line around the outside of the wobbly balls to indicate the leaves. Then draw a woody texture on the trunk and branches. Add a few small twigs.

Grass

To show someone standing on grass, draw a jagged line to show blades of grass covering the bottom of the shoe.

Or draw the grass more detailed, like this.

For detailed grass, draw a row of separate blades like this. It will usually look better if a few of them are bent over.

Then add another row behind it, and another, and keep adding rows until you've filled the grass area.

Use three or four different greens, to fill in the vertical lines of grass. Try to color a few of the blades completely, but not all of them. The inked lines will separate the blades.

Dirt is simple to draw. Start with some cracks, and a few ovals for pebbles. Then color in the dirt using a medium brown. Finally, use a dark brown for the shadows and to add interest.

Sitting and Lying Down

Posture is very important when characters are sitting down. Try drawing your characters sitting in different positions to see which suits them best.

This character looks unhappy. He's bent over, leaning on his elbows, with his head in his hands. He is either bored or sad.

Here is a formal pose. This character's feet are set slightly apart. His back is straight, and his hands are on his lap.

This pose is much more relaxed and informal. He is slouching and leaning back, with his feet apart. His hands are behind his head, which makes him look relaxed. Perhaps he is daydreaming?

This girl is definitely not relaxed. Her legs and arms are crossed and held close to her body, which usually shows that someone is nervous or upset.

When a character hugs her knees to her chest, she looks sad. Looking away, with eyes closed also shows a character is upset.

Here she is leaning forward and looking at someone. This makes her look more enthusiastic, as well as a little impatient.

Now that you've tried some different ways of sitting, what is your characters sitting on?

Furniture

Chairs are simple to draw. Start off with a box with an extended back.

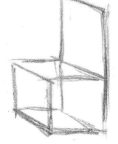

Add the details. This chair has straight, round legs and a very straight back and seat, all formed from cylinders and boxes.

For a different style, round off the corners of the seat and back. Then, add pillows. Draw the legs angled, as long as they end on the bottom surface of the box.

Draw more complicated chairs, like a swivel chair, by using boxes and tubes. Or you can draw really complicated seats like the science-fiction-styled chair.

This sci-fi chair may look complicated, but it is made of basic shapes, with a lot of details added. The back of the chair is drawn at an angle. The arms, as well as the wires and pillows, are added at the end.

41

Characters can sit on the floor, too. A character who is sitting cross-legged, like Drei, looks calm but a little formal. Kara's pose, leaning back on her arms with one leg bent, is much more relaxed.

Try drawing your characters sitting on the floor in different ways. Here are some stick figures to give you more pose ideas.

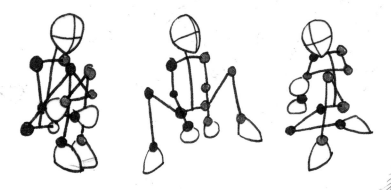

Try drawing your character lying down. This pose is like standing. However, when a character is lying on his or her side, the character's legs will be close together. The character's arms are resting on the surface.

Here is a character carrying another character.

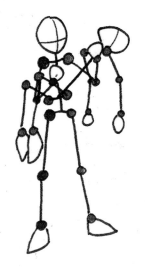

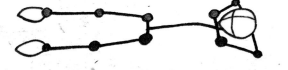

Running and Jumping

Now for some real action!

Basic running looks like this.

Of course, not everyone runs the same way. Pick a few poses from the stick figures and try them with your own characters.

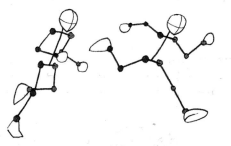

See how the boy with the red hair seems to be running faster than the boy with the blue hair? Depending on which pose you pick, and how you draw the pose, your character seems to be running. Show movement by drawing your character's clothes and hair being blown back.

When you are drawing characters running on a background, add shadows to show a character's feet have left the ground.

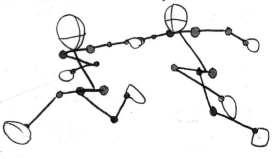

You can draw characters jumping, too. Someone jumping up might look something like this. Just remember the basic shapes.

Change the running action to show someone jumping farther.

Show movement with speed lines. These work best in small pictures and are simple to draw. Just draw and ink your character. Then draw a lot of parallel lines of different thicknesses in the direction of the movement, as in the picture right.

Use a ruler for this. If you have trouble keeping all of the lines going in the same direction, draw them in pencil first. Measure each line to make sure it is parallel. Then make sure each line goes in the same direction as the closest pencil line.

If you don't want to use speed lines, there are other ways to show movement.

For the foot on the left, draw a broken outline and turn it into some lines going in the direction of the movement.

The second, scratchy foot shows the best method to use if you're not planning to color in your drawing. It seems blurred, with broken and "ghost" outlines, and the shading of the foot leaves a trail of lines. These lines of shading all go in the direction of the movement, like speed lines.

Fighting

Drawing fights is a little tricky at first, but with practice you'll be able to master these techniques. One of the best ways of getting ideas is to watch a martial art like karate, jujitsu, or kick-boxing.

One of the first things you learn in martial arts is a basic fighting stance, like Drei is using here.

There are a lot of other, more decorative stances that look really cool. Try drawing your characters in different stances.

Drawing a basic punch looks like this.

Your character doesn't have to stand in a normal fighting stance to punch. It's up to you how he or she stands. Then put in some lines to show where the movement is, as well as a little jagged shape to show where he or she is hitting.

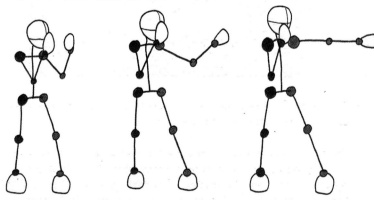

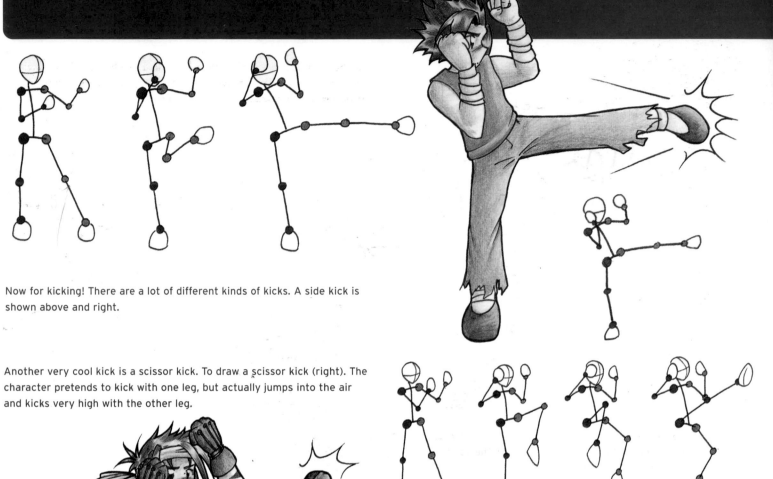

Now for kicking! There are a lot of different kinds of kicks. A side kick is shown above and right.

Another very cool kick is a scissor kick. To draw a scissor kick (right). The character pretends to kick with one leg, but actually jumps into the air and kicks very high with the other leg.

Don't forget to draw the left or right arms and legs punching or kicking.

Use "action lines," when a character gets hit. An action line is a curve drawn before drawing a stick figure to show the character's movement, balance, or how he or she bends. If a character is hit very hard in the lower chest or stomach, he or she will usually bend over.

If a character is hit higher up, he or she is knocked backward. Show how hard someone is hit by the character's reaction, expression, and the movement of the character's clothes and hair.

Show an impact by drawing a jagged shape like this.

But some people prefer to use lots of lines pointing toward the impact point, like this.

In small drawings, show how hard a character has been hit by using speed lines. Leave a gap in the speed lines level with the point of impact for a dramatic effect.

Draw impact lines like those below with a ruler so they all point to a dot in the middle of the impact point. Press much lighter the nearer to the impact point to draw attention to it. Make the expression on the character's face look like the person's been hit really hard.

Animals

Animals and fantasy creatures are popular in Manga and Anime. They are drawn the same way as people, using basic shapes.

Real Animals

To see how easy it is, try drawing a basic cat.

1. Start off by drawing a circle for the head and two overlapping circles for the body. Add tubes for the legs and an oval for the top of the back legs. Draw a long sausage shape for the tail. Now draw some guidelines on the head, just like you did for your character's face.

2. Draw a bump for the muzzle (the mouth and nose area). Add some pointed eyes and ears and rounded shapes for the paws. Draw around the outside of the body circles and part of the head circle.

3. Draw the mouth and nose. Add details to the eyes and ears. Draw toes on the paws. Then draw a more jagged line around the body to show the fur. Add whiskers, too. Darken the lines you want to keep.

4. Now ink it.

5. Next, add color. Use a dark orange first, in the direction of the fur, leaving a lot of gaps. Then go over the dark-orange areas with a bright orange, pressing harder. Shade the lighter areas with yellow.

It's easy to change this cat into another kind of animal. Perhaps you would prefer to draw a dog instead of a cat?

1. The shapes for cats and dogs are similar, but draw longer shapes for a dog's body and more pointed egg shape for the head. Make the tail shorter, wider, and more pointed, too.

2. Make the muzzle a little longer. Draw the dog's eyes rounder, and its ears floppy and bent over. The tail is drawn with a lot of fur.

3. Now add the details. The mouth is bigger and longer than a cat's. Make sure the legs are longer so the body is farther from the ground. Draw a collar as well.

4. Once you've added the details, ink in your drawing.

5. Now color it in. Use a much smoother coloring technique because this dog has shorter, smoother fur.

You can draw a lot of other animals just by changing the basic shapes. See if you can copy some of these animals. Try looking at photographs to get ideas for more animals.

Wings are a lot of fun to draw.

You don't just have to draw real animals. It is really fun to make up your own creatures. Try drawing a creature with dragonlike wings.

1 Start by drawing rounded triangle shapes. The wing on the left is curved around, and the one on the right is open.

1 Start by drawing the same shapes you used for the feathered wings.

2 Divide the wings into two parts. The part that will be closest to the bird's body has smaller feathers. Draw the basic shapes of the longer feathers in the other part.

2 Add pointed lines to the spurs of the wings.

3 Draw the smaller feathers using rows of pointed "U" shapes. Add tufts of feathers where the wings join the body. Make the corners of the wings a little jagged too. Now go around the lines you want to keep so you see them better.

3 Add a ball and a curved triangle at the corners of the wings for talons. Draw U-shaped curves to create the wings' membranes.

4 Ink and color in the wings. Add shadows where each feather comes out from under the one above it to make them stand out from each other. Lighter blue is a great color for the shadows.

4 Ink and color in the wings. Go around the pointed lines with purple, not black. Shade the membranes a darker color near the spurs to show the curves.

There are lots of different ways to draw animal features.

Eyes can be simple, complicated, round, or pointed. They can even be drawn like a human eye.

Here are some ideas for animal mouths and noses.

There are many ideas for drawing different kinds of ears, paws, and tails. Try drawing features together to see what weird creatures you create!

Try drawing a dragon.

 Draw an egg shape for the head, a round body, and a long neck and tail. The dragon has long feet and little arms, so make sure your shapes show that. Draw one of the wings, too.

 Add the details. Give the dragon pointed toes and little, pointed fingers. Draw the other wing and add the spurs. A long, pointed snout looks cool. This dragon has narrow, slanted eyes and a V-shaped crest on its head. Smooth out the body shape.

With the basics done, now add the finishing touches. Draw whiskers around the nostril, a row of spiked scales down the back, and a pointed fin on the end of the tail. Draw some big scales on the belly and in a line around the snout. Finish the wings and then go around the lines that you want to keep.

Ink and color in your dragon. Try using two different greens, a warm yellow, and a bright blue for the eyes. To draw the finer scales on the body, color the main green. Then add lots of rows of "U" shapes with a darker green.

Coloring

Coloring in your character gives it a lot of life. Colored pencils are great because each one lets you draw a range of light and dark shades.

Draw a character to color in. Here is a fluffy creature.

Pick the first color. In this case, the creature is going to be red. Color very lightly because this is the lightest color. Keep your pencil sharp and at an angle. Working quick and lightly in one direction.

Use the same pencil, but color harder over most of the drawing. Leave the areas that would receive the most light pale. Work in a different direction from the first layer. For a smoother look, use a lot of light layers going in different directions instead of one heavy one. Blend the light and medium tones smoothly into one another.

Use either the same pencil, or a darker pencil. Work in the areas that are in shadow to make them darker. Color lightly near the medium tones so the shadows blend in with the colors you've already done.

Repeat this process with each color. To make your coloring look smooth and bright, go over the colors with a white or pale-colored pencil, pressing very hard. This will blend the different colors.

To make your creature furrier, add lines in the direction of the fur with the medium and dark tones. Then go over the area very hard with the light color.

Now that you know some coloring techniques, make your creatures look the way you like. The boy on the right has a whole bunch of weird animals with him. The basic shapes used to create them are shown below. See if you can draw them. Then come up with your own animals to draw and color.

Here is a magical creature for Kara.

The creature has blue and white feathered wings. His body is bright green to make him look unusual and to make him stand out. He also has big, bright, red-pink eyes to contrast with his fur. Try designing an animal friend for one of your characters.

Now that you've designed some characters and creatures, try putting them in different poses and backgrounds.

55

Putting it All Together

Now you have your characters, but what are you going to do with them? In this chapter, make a full-page picture with them. You can either follow the instructions exactly, using Drei and Kara, or follow the same process using your own characters.

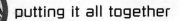
▶▶

When thinking about a full-page picture, it's a good idea to jot down some ideas on a bit of spare paper. Draw some boxes that are the same shape as your paper and draw little composition sketches to see how you're going to fit your characters on the page. These are called "thumbnail sketches," and are really handy to make sure you fit everything on the page. It is very difficult if you get halfway through a drawing, and have to erase it because something important won't fit on the page.

Try several compositions. When you've found a design you like, make sure you have all of the paper, pencils, erasers, pens, coloring pencils, and pencil sharpener you need. You may need a ruler, a few colored pens, some white paint, and a thin paintbrush. It will be helpful for you to have a big, hardback book or a smooth board to lean on. So think of an idea, get your stuff together, and let's go!

Pencils

1 Start your drawing with the character that is in front.

2 Build up the body by drawing basic shapes like tubes, boxes, and circles on top of the stick figure.

3 Draw your other characters' stick figures and basic shapes.

4 Start adding the details. Start with the faces and hands and smooth out the bodies, arms, and legs.

5 Add the hair and clothes, and don't forget to show them being blown by movement. Draw folds or creases in the clothes to make them look realistic. Draw in the rest of the facial details.

6 Draw in fine details like belts, buttons, shoe laces, and decoration.

7 Start drawing the background. A wall makes a great background. It shows the characters nicely. If you draw bricks, use a ruler to make your grid.

8 Finish the background. Add the bricks and the sun. Drew the edge of the ground, a railing, and the sea (which should always be horizontal). If they are smudged or faint, go over the characters' lines a little harder.

Inking ▶▶

9 This is a complicated picture, so look at the inking in more detail. Start by using a medium-sized pen for most of the regular lines. Start with Kara and her creature, inking in most of her skin, clothes, and hair. Leave out the very fine details for now.

10 Finish inking your characters' lines with the medium-sized pen. Then use a fine pen for details like eyes, noses, and mouths. Used a thin pen for the details on the ears and the trim of Kara's shirt.

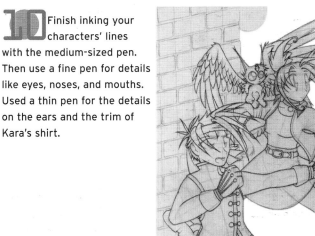

11 To make your characters stand out from the background, use a thin pen to ink the background. Once you have inked everything, start to erase the pencil lines.

12 Your picture should look like this. To make things stand out better, add more details.

13 Draw around the outside of your characters with a thicker pen to make them stand out. Because Drei is in front of Kara, use an even thicker pen for him. Fill in the shadows of the eyes and add a few shadows with your thinnest pen.

Once you've done that, it's time to color in!

Coloring

14 Start by adding the base colors to the background. The ground is concrete, so color it with a warm gray. On the wall, use a light yellow-brown for the mortar and a light red-orange for the bricks.

15 Finish off the main colors of the background, with a dark blue for the sea and a light one for the sky. Make the sun yellow and orange, and the rail bright green. Add any necessary textures. The brick texture with a dark, red-brown is shown on page 36.

16 Now, decide on the skin color of your characters. Start coloring the skin. Use either a very pale base color, use the color of the paper as a base on which to build the skin's mid-tones and shadows.

17 Next, color the hair. Leave plenty of jagged highlights to make it look shiny. Make sure all of your lines go in the hair direction. If you want the hair to look shinier, go over the color with a white pencil to blend the colors into the highlights. Once the hair is done, it's time to color any very pale or white areas. This may sound silly, but white objects shouldn't be all-white in color because they have shadows. It's good to use a color like a very pale blue, gray-green, or purple for the shadows instead of gray, because grays make things look dull. Purples look warmer, and blues look cooler.

poses & action    animals   putting it all together

18 Start coloring the clothes. Lay down a base color for all of Kara's clothes.

Then add the mid-tones and shadows.

19 Next, color in most of Drei's clothes, leaving the metallic areas for later.

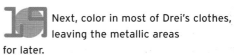

20 Color any metallic or shiny objects and the trim on Drei's shirt, his gloves, and Kara's jewelry. Give the animal's feathers blue tips.

21 Finish the main areas of color. If any characters have their mouths open, color the inside of their mouths.

Now it's time to do the eyes. Using a dark color, begin shading smoothly from the top of the iris.

Press hard using a bright color over that,

Now we're almost done. Add some red around the area above the noses to show the blush. Draw some red blush lines, too. Now draw Drei's pointed blue markings with a dark-blue pen. Add any details you didn't want to outline in black.

If you want to give your drawing a little extra shine, use white paint and a thin brush to add some highlights to the eyes and any shiny surfaces. Add a lot of dots of light to the metallic parts of Drei's clothes.

 And you're finished!

Final Thoughts...

Now that you've seen the steps that go into making a full-page color drawing of original characters, it's time to try it with your own ideas and characters.

As you've seen, it's easy and fun to think of your own original characters and pictures.
• Start out with a character concept.
• Try different faces and body shapes until you find a look you like and that suits the personality of your character.
• Try different costumes until you find one that fits how you want your character to dress.
• Think of things for your character to do, and about what his or her posture should be.
• Draw the character as much as you want!

Your character can be anyone and do anything. The only limit to your character is your imagination. When you have a character, think of what his or her family, friends, and enemies are. Think up stories and consider how your characters act around each other. Decide what the characters' world is like. With a little time, effort, and imagination, you can create a whole cast of characters for your own Manga-and Anime-style universes. The possibilities are endless!

So what are you waiting for? Grab some paper, a pencil, and your idea, and get creative. And have fun!

Credits

This book is dedicated to all the wonderful people who have supported, inspired, and cheered me on when I've needed it.

Most of you know who you are, and I don't have room to name you all, but (in no particular order); Mum and Dad - For...well, everything, really. Jack "Dave" James - You're fantastic. I hope you like your squirrel. Chandra, Kitty, Abby, Dave and Lynne - For inspiring me and keeping me sane as well as being the generally brilliant people that you are. Sam,

Dean, Sel, Jess, Liam, Hayley, Philip, Tom, Neil, and the gang - I love you all. David and Sarah - For making this possible a second time.

And last, but not least, to everyone who has e-mailed and written to me to show that what I've done has been worth it.

Index